MIGRATION

Ann Clayton

Clayton, Ann
    Migration / Ann Clayton

Poems.
ISBN: 978-1-928171-55-3 (pbk)
ISBN: 978-1-928171-56-0 (ebk)

Copyright © Ann Clayton, 2017

Cover image: "Impossible Journey", by David Wilhelm

Vocamus Community Publications

130 Dublin Street North
Guelph, Ontario
N1H 4N4

Table of Contents

Being Here	1
Mountains of Memory	4
Sanskrit	5
Tableau Vivant	6
Canadian Yarn: A Villanelle	7
The Child	8
Poem for a Canadian	9
Doves on Johnston Green	11
The Bridges of Ontario	12
The New Canadian Gardener	14
Driving to Kitchener, Late December	16
Kitchener Oktoberfest	17
Grammar	18
Guelph: Late Summer	19
On the Sitges Train	21
Man of My Dreams	22
Forsythia in New York	24
This Fall, Walking to the Downtown	27
Praise-Poem	28
Migration	30
Biographical Note	31

Being Here

Here is no easy place to be.
Here there is restlessness,
rocking on a sea, bumping against
a wooden jetty, the water choppy.
In Cape Town Maria de la Quellerie
guards the viaduct, a little further in
from her stony husband, guardian
of the VOC, hat and cane rakish.
If you wander up the Heerengracht
you will reach the Botanic Gardens
planted like the Dias crosses
at the Cape of Good Hope.
Some of the trees are old, hard as rock,
almost artefact. There will be
Japanese tourists near the goldfish
ponds, smiling into cameras.
Old, poor people, often reading,
will sit on park benches;
small grey squirrels run and raise
their paws, tails in a flourish.
The Houses of Parliament are gracious
looking, absorbed into an adjacent
broad gravel avenue, where you will
often meet a face you knew before.
None of this tells the truth
of history, though it remains
and seems to tell the story.
The real tale needs another tongue.
To be translated into snow
is to know differently, that
democracy is both word and thing,
a slow dialogue between people.
Here there were once pioneers, too:

voyageurs, farmers, priests,
war brides, governors, gentlewomen,
starving Irish, European artisans
who built the Toronto viaduct
and where a nun once fell.
Now the city rises: blue grass,
railway lines, industrial sprawl
not unlike Johannesburg
if you forget the mine-dumps
now rehabilitating into green.
Toronto has more churches,
choirs, galleries, and McDonald's.
Body and soul can be fed.
In Johannesburg there are more dead
and their cries are in the air.
Street pedlars sell oranges to the poor;
the city slides toward Diagonal Street,
the glassy Stock Exchange, the Market
Theatre, where multiracial jubilation
rises like a fountain from the past.
And here in this Ontario town
three stone figures sprial from a pool
outside a bus shelter and a bank.
The parents lift a stone infant
and, slowly, they all oxidize in spray.
This is a town where I learned to pray
because all other sources failed.
And so I have to stay.
Not because a God is here
who is not elsewhere, but because
the flower that grows here
is now wound around my heart.
It is the iron flower of freedom

and of history, of the country
that I left, and the one that I have found.
History is the lie of the land.
And in the Botanic Gardens
there are iron railings and sunny paths;
bright birds shuffle in their cages;
underwater, goldfish flicker, visible, then lost.

Mountains of Memory

Table Mountain leans in grey majesty
over the city, shrouded in wispy mist,
dwarfing and cradling the town;
to the right the lion sleeps.
Driving toward the mountain
through the Flats' industrial sprawl –
Devil's Peak spires on the left,
grainy surfaces a cratered moon.
Deer roam at Rhodes Memorial,
sunlight on those peaceful slopes.
Cape Flats, Guguletu, Nyanga:
apartheid's cruel geography.
Tables with chicken wings for sale
under blue-gums, shanties, sparse bush,
boys dicing in red dust at the station.
Salt River, Observatory, Mowbray,
Rosebank, Rondebosch, Newlands,
all stations to Simonstown;
toy train curving between sea and coast
past shuttered bungalows at St James:
boys heading for the surf.
All the stations of my youth.
The litany of memory,
the rosary to tell lost time
over, hold the beads in my hand
so that I know well what it is
I am letting go: that bright bay
where the southeaster blows,
flower-sellers plump in Adderley St,
Coloured women hurling their wit
like brave streamers into wind.
Hold them all against my heart:
my people, my places, lost and found,
over and over again, until time ceases.

Sanskrit

Small people, their talk
all clicks and chatter,
hunters, speeding through bush,
impala, sand and rock.

Poison in their arrows
that fly to their mark,
the ostrich shell their gourd,
survival was their work.

Existence was their art:
the fleeting figures of the day
mirrored on the cave wall;
the hunt, the mystery, heart.

Some say they were tranced
as they painted: ochre, red,
brown hunters and hunted.
Some say they danced.

I miss them, though they were gone
almost before I was conceived.
Small relic bands may still roam
the Kalahari, drink from an African stream.

Their art survives: an African dream.
I want to live in their cave.

Tableau Vivant

For Steven Biko

I have in mind an evening tableau.
It is the karoo, at dusk. It insists.
The light is violet, almost solid.
The air is cool, like stone.
I am that stone.

This picture will not go away.
The veld is open to the night sky;
a dassie scurries somewhere.
The koppies are silent;
I see them there.

This vision takes the place of something.
It fills an absence, like smoke,
Lacan would say a lack.
It rushes in where presence was,
a place the eyes could see.

Evening air is cooling stone.
Purple light pours down.
God painted the sky.
The karoo borders infinity.

Canadian Yarn: A Villanelle

*For Can Themba, Bloke Modisane,
Todd Matshikiza, and Nat Nakasa*

This is a tale that needs to be told:
I left my old world and found a new.
The wound went through me like a sword.

White snow is now my own free word;
the forest marches on and through,
and yet this tale does need to be told.

Love is the hearth when winds blow cold:
it takes a bow, it speaks on cue.
The wound went through me like a sword.

I left my mother, brother, and kraal;
I found new people, nation, an igloo.
This is a tale that needs to be told.

Love is a birthright that cannot be sold.
My heart is in this barn with me and you;
the wound went through me like a sword.

Home is here now; home is what I hold
while birds fly upward into blue.
This is a tale that needs to be told;
the wound went through me like a sword.

The Child

Translation from Ingrid Jonker

The child is not dead
the child lifts his fist to his mother
who shouts Africa shouts the smell
of freedom and veld
in the townships of the barricaded heart.

The child lifts his fist to his father
in the march of generations
who shout Africa shout the smell
of justice and blood
in the streets of his fighting pride.

The child is not dead
not at Langa not at Nyanga
not at Orlando not at Sharpeville
not at Philippi police station
where he lies with a bullet in his head.

The child is the shadow of the soldiers
on guard with guns saracens and batons
the child is present in all convocations and
legislations
the child peers through the windows of houses and
into the hearts
of mothers
the child who wanted to play in the sun in Nyanga is
everywhere
the child grown a man treks through all of Africa
the child grown a giant travels all the world

without a pass.

Poem for a Canadian

I don't know how I came to love you.

It had something to do with the silence
around your room, that first time,
jutting like a ship's prow into forest,
the branches softened and thickened by quiet snow.

The silence of your being there, with me.

I don't know how I came to love you.

It had something to do with ice-hockey on TV:
those gladiators gliding with burdened grace over ice
and their staccato scores on the radio.

It had something to do with standing
on a high, precarious bridge in Barcelona,
a gaudy work by Gaudi, feeling dizzy
with the flu, and knowing I could lean
against you.

You kneeled at the tourist kiosk, pretending
to be a dwarf, and I laughed, later.

Your jokes have a long slow fuse
and I usually enjoy the final explosion.

I'm not at all sure how I came to love you.

It must surely have been related to lust:
to falling greedily upon each other's
flesh, all that thrusting, stroking, and
the final kiss, as if we could devour
all we knew of as the past.

It must have been your longed-for letters
with the news of your daily life, so far away
in that same snow that now mantles me,
in these forests, now become my home.

It must have been your patient gifts
of kindness and love, your readiness to be
surprised, as I am, by the randomness
of everything we are, as lovers,
finding our wisdom, and our peace, here.

And today again the snow is falling:
thick, mantling, silencing, white.

Soon I will go out and begin my day.

I will await with you the everlasting light.

Doves on Johnston Green

Doves are the souls of the dead.

If you see a fleet of doves, descended,
they are our parents, and our children.

They do not speak. Their silence
is the essence of their beauty.

Sometimes a whole section will lift,
a raft on a heavy swell.

One or two take to flight,
unannounced. The rest look cryptic

as if considering their plans.
Their feathers ruff about their necks;

for a moment they most resemble
digruntled Elizabethans, courtiers

who do not know when the monarch
may once more take to beheadings.

Their presence is vast and tranquil
on the grass. They substitute

for humans, but closer to the ground.
Their graceful blessing makes no sound

in this green quadrangle of angels.

The Bridges of Ontario

So much love has flowed
under these bridges
of Ontario
and along the winding
Grand River
which loops about
and between
these single and twin towns
flooding into fullness
when you least expect it.
So much blood has flowed
under these bridges
of Ontario
into the branching candelabra
of Mennonite clans –
canny, heimische people
who quilt, bake
and strike hard bargains.
So much water has flowed
under these bridges
of Ontario
and blood is thicker than water.
Corn is sold
as peaches and cream
in Ontario
and at the market
there are treasures to be found
though you have to search for them.
The broad fields of brown loam
lie open to the sky
in Ontario
and at Halloween
pumpkins and ghosts consort

together in the fields.
This is God's acre.
It brings forth its harvest
in due course
with patient tilling
always depending on God's weather.
So much blood has flowed
under these covered, kissing bridges
of Ontario.

The New Canadian Gardener

For Ernest Hemingway

In Canada the garden is not the yard
and the yard is not the garden, either.

And the yard is not the dusty space
behind a whitewashed house with a zinc roof
that you sweep with a straw broom
bought from a woman who arrived
at your gate, baby and brooms on her back
and who smiled radiantly when you bought one.

I'm not sure what the yard is,
in Canada. It's not the long piece
of fabric you cut from a bolt
of cloth, either, since metrication.
It's just the ground you own
(I guess) usually covered with snow.

And in that Canadian yard
you can put something, called a garden,
in, but not before Victoria Day
very late in May, in case of further
frost, or snow, or other precipitation.

This garden is not something
that can be counted upon
around the year, obviously,
mainly because you can't see it
under all that snow.

This garden you put in
is something which excites people
in the spring, a short season of a few days.
It could be flowers, or vegetables,
as in 'vegetable garden'.

A garden is something that flourishes
briefly, during summer,
which lasts for June and July.
Then you can watch that garden
fall, or you can take it out, or in,
and wait for the following spring.

No-one in their right mind
would choose to be a Canadian
gardener.

I think, if I ever own a house,
I'll just call my yard, a garden.

And I'll plant Canadian wildflowers and
soft grasses, and wheatgrass with a green, sharp
stubble under it, like a man's three-day beard,
which I saw greening the wheatfields along
Highway 7, last weekend, and fields of soft brown grass
which looked as though bodies had been lying there
lovingly, bending that soft grass back, and fields of
short golden cornstalks, which I would call mielie
fields, all that soft mixed beauty along the highway
that I saw

And then I might call myself a Canadian gardener
and I would call that garden good.

Driving to Kitchener, Late December

On the left
fields of snow and farm,
on the right, corn.

This is the season
when Christ was born.

The sinuous road coils
between winter's paradox.

In the stall the manger
and the cattle, warm.

Kitchener Oktoberfest

For Vojtech and Mirka

Soft leaves sift
into stuffed scarecrows
on steep side streets.

Unemployed, their straw heads
drift and dream
of autumn.

Amber-umber, yellow, russet-
red; their feet made
of striped socks, crossed.

Peeling paint on neglected
wooden porch; street sales
of hand-me-downs glitter

from Yugoslavia, Mexico,
Italy, Africa, Slovakia:
give a penny, take a penny.

Autumn's abundance everywhere:
gold scattered on the earth.
God's harvest every year

since the fall of Berlin

takes these strangers in.

Grammar

So much speech
in a bird's black eye.

"I did not appear
to bother you. I came
to see you enjoy that
ice-cream on this bench.

I'm pleased it's good.

And now I'm just
strolling around you
without saying a word

and soon I'll be gone,
but I'm pleased to see
you're quite OK.

I wasn't looking for a hand-out,
either. Don't get me wrong.
Though you might have spared me
the end of that sugar cone."

All of that talk
in a white bird's eye
and singular, delicate,
syntactic walk.

Guelph: Late Summer

After Rilke's "Herbsttag"

Home is where I am.
Heart-whole, holding off harm.

Here is where I live.
Earth-bound, aspiring to fly.

There is only the one sky.
Birds semaphore across it.

What they encode is the fall,
leaf-turning, the delayed sound of the axe
thudding into wood across the river.

There is only an edge of amber now:
a russet thread pulling through green.

These trees arch over spaces I have been.
Our lives run beneath.
Fresh-cut lawn grass falls in swathes.

Distant sound of traffic and river,
wood-pecker's attack, cardinal's call.

Cladding is stripped from the new
civic centre. Old bridges fall.

The wood was rotten, the edges
dangerous.

I look forward to a new bridge
in the old place. The ducks don't care.
They forage in the shadow under willows.

This is my life in a new land;
I have come to the end of fear.

In the night you sweat it out,
like malaria, or yellow fever.

The flowers consumed their own bounty.

The carnival is over.

On the Sitges Train

On the Sitges train

your fingers pink with strawberries –

love's stolen fruit –

you made your coat a pillow

for my heavy head

and the day's day-dream

on the Sitges train

with you.

Man of My Dreams

My lover is a janitor:
he looks after buildings
when all the workers are gone.
He switches off the lights,
saves on water bills,
and goes to market
early in the morning.

He can blow smoke circles
without blinking.
He can juggle several balls in the air
while smiling.

He's tall as a bolt
of black cloth
though every other day
he appears as a dancing dwarf.

His toenail clippings
fly all over the room
like small shards of shrapnel.

His dental floss is green.

He has an old-fashioned car
but dresses like a spiv.

He isn't all men to me.
He's very singular.

I don't know why
I like him so much.

It could be a trick
of the light
on certain days
in the early Ontario winter

when the horizon flushes
with cold along the dusk

that makes me think
this love could last

if I could only learn
to whistle
like a man

and he could learn
that I am only
the woman I am

and these poems
are paper planes

that could teach
us both
to fly.

Forsythia in New York

I remember the swollen
yellow buds and blooms
of forsythia in New York
and the sharp cold of the street
in spring.

A small hotel room
where we explored
all the spaces that there were.
The walls receded. I uncoiled.

Police sirens pulsed in the night-
time streets, just like the sit-coms,
as if they were street-legal
and street-wise.
Cagney and Lacey were there.

I got sold dud batteries
and saw a drunkard hustled
in a gutter. The fuzz arrived.

We beetled along below
skyscrapers, in the newness
of new love: strangers, lovers,
lovers, strangers. Handy-dandy.

Love made that ugly, bountiful,
swarming, siren city my home.

I wore a corduroy tie
that you knitted
into a feminine knot.

Or so you said. It could
have been a Canadian Boy Scout
knot, for all I knew.

You walked along the edge
of the pavement, as gentlemen
should. There were no carriages
nor puddles, and no crinolines.
But I liked your doing it.

Liberty was there, arm nobly
upraised, in her spiky crown,
benevolently gazing down
on Staten Island and the ferry.

Cars were a nuisance in New York,
you said, not to mention the expense.
Canada was a lot cheaper, and a lot
better. I believed you.

We scoffed our lunch with tourists
at the top of the Empire State.
It was a bit like being at sea,
the vista and sway of it.

If you paid a foreign coin
you could gaze through
a telescope at the urbanscape.

So we did, standing on either side,
as if we indulged a young child,
together. Suddenly everything was fine.

I did not know then,
how long the view would be
nor how high the cost.
If I had, I might have lost heart.

But I could not lose my heart.
You already had that as a gift
outright, a pledge to be held
in trust, against all the twists
and knots of pain, which were
not in view, that day.

Golden forsythia in cold New York:
splinters of glass in the heart,
and underneath, a world unfurling.

This Fall, Walking to the Downtown

"The world is charged with the grandeur of God."
– Gerard Manley Hopkins

Suddenly leaves lie
thick as thought.
The trees have dropped
their brains to the ground
and stare empty-headed
at the sky.
It seemed to happen overnight.
I must have been asleep.
You can't walk without
kicking up a ruckus of leaves:
dry, light, and brittle.
They're the dead skin
of this past summer
that left too soon.
I'm tired of time's tricks and cyclical habits,
its way of disappearing
with my life.
I must have thought
summer would go on forever
but now there's a breeze
brisk as a broom
sweeping up neighbours
at street corners.
Love will have to do
in place of leaves.

Praise-Poem

Mandela is the father of the people.
He fathered freedom in South Africa.
Now his hair is saying "white!"
His children walk the world.

Mandela is a Transkei child.
That is where he grew and played,
herding cattle, under the sun.
He learned to be a patient man
in Transkei, South Africa.

Mandela is the one who knows
about prison walls in Pretoria,
Pollsmoor, Robben Island.
He could not swim away.
He learned to load gravel.

Mandela was a boxer.
He gave the Afrikaners
a knockout blow.
The people cheered. The referee
counted to ten. Those Nats were out cold.

Mandela turned that cell
into a cathedral. It became a huge temple
for all the people who found freedom
in South Africa, and all over the world.
They walked in its beautiful light.

Now this Transkei child is known
everywhere. This herder of cattle walks
with kings and queens. They bow down
and say: thank you, Mandela
for you gave us freedom.

You gave us freedom
to be men and women,
not serfs and underlings.
You fathered new, proud people
who could walk around the world.

Praises to the name and family of Mandela.
We are all sprung from this patient man
who turned the whole world into a church
where we could become ourselves, where
we could become silent, and pray for peace.

We pray for the herders of cattle
and those who live in cities
and remember the price that was paid.
It was a kind of lobola for freedom.
The price was time and long years.

God bless South Africa in its new freedom.
We remember those who made it free.
They were in prison, but they made us free
all around the world. People became equal.
We thank this Transkei child, a herder of cattle.

Migration

There is no end to the letting go
the travelling and enfolding
of memory into place, my will
broken into peace by endless withholding
time flowing a river backward
I did not know I had crossed
until my feet found the ground
of this new land, silence and plenty.

There is no end to the finding
the mining of the past, an ore
veined with blood, assembling
in new formations, the lore
of the elders, gifts I never knew
I owned until I opened
my hand and saw their wealth
unclasped, endless love, unbound.

There is no end to the salutation
of a continent, its mountains, cities,
forests, lakes, chequered farms,
pastures, animals, ploughs, spires,
the habitants of history, arms
tensed against the river's current,
their guarded faces and bright feathers
as they sail over the dark to shining water.

Biographical Note

Ann Clayton was a teacher of Commonwealth literature at the University of Guelph and the University of Waterloo. She was a teacher of literature at universities in Johannnesburg, South Africa, where she also worked as a writer, free lance journalist and book reviewer.

Her critical articles on literature, arts, culture, and politics have appeared in South African, Canadian and international newspapers and journals. She has published three book-length academic titles: *Olive Schreiner: A Casebook* (McGraw-Hill); *Women and Writing in South Africa: A Critical Anthology* (Heinemann); *Olive Schreiner* (Twayne). She has also published two previous volumes of poetry: *Leaving Home* (Red Kite / Snailpress) and *Eternal Day* (Drum Media).

www.ingramcontent.com/pod-product-compliance
Lightning Source LLC
Chambersburg PA
CBHW032005060426
42449CB00031B/810